SANTA'S

God

A Children's Fable about
the Biggest Question Ever

NEALE DONALD WALSCH

Illustrations by Em Claire

an *EmNin* book

Santa's God
A Children's Fable about the Biggest Question Ever

Neale Donald Walsch

Original Story: Neale Donald Walsch.
Story adaptations: Neale Donald Walsch and Em Claire
Illustrations: Em Claire
Cover design: Frame 25 Productions
Interior Book Design: Frame 25 Productions and Em Claire
Colored Pencil Work: Beth Stark
Illustration reproductions/enhancement: Goldie Schemanski-Irelock Imaging; www.Irelock.com
The sketches of Santa statues in this book were based on
original Pipka Santa figurines and are presented here with permission.
More information on these collectibles may be found at www.Pipka.com.

EmNin Books
PMB 1144
1257 Siskiyou Blvd
Ashland, OR 97520
e-mail: emninbooks@aol.com

ISBN 978-1-57174-596-5

Distributed by:
Hampton Roads Publishing Company, Inc.
PO Box 8107
Charlottesville, VA 22906

434-296-2772
fax: 703-637-1322
e-mail: hrpc@hrpub.com
www.hrpub.com

10 9 8 7 6 5 4 3 2 1
Printed on acid-free paper in China

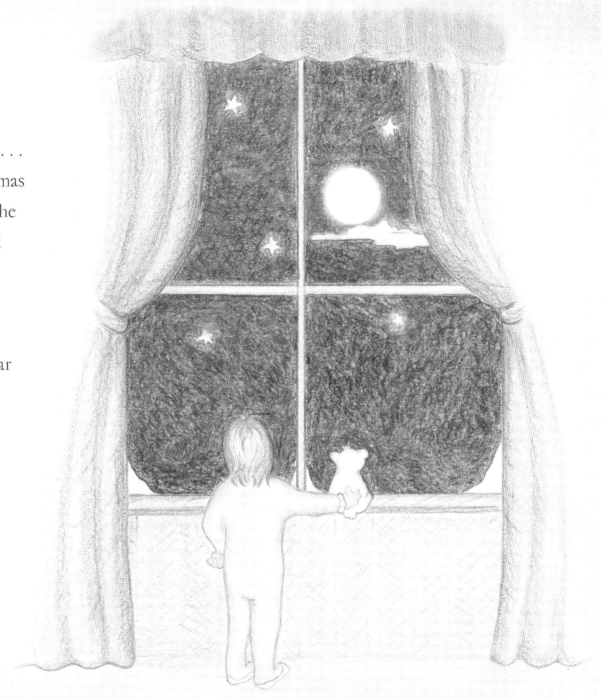

It was the middle of the night . . . not just *any* night, but Christmas Eve . . . and Melinda was at the window, searching the sky and trying as hard as she could to stay awake.

She was determined that this year she was *not going to fall asleep!* This year she was going to see him if it was the last thing she ever did!

So naturally her ears perked
up when she heard a *thud!*
She ran down the
stairs and there he was!
Right in front of her!
SANTA CLAUS!

"I knew you were real!" she said, a lot louder than she wanted to. "I just *knew* it!"

"Well, of course I am," Santa chuckled as he turned around to look at her. He didn't even seem surprised that Melinda was awake. "Want to come on down from the stairs and have a nice visit?"

"Wow, yes!" Melinda giggled, and she scampered over to give Santa a great big hug.

"You act like you were
expecting me!" she said.
"I was!" Santa replied.
"You were?"
"I sure was. Every year I pick out one child to talk with
when I visit all the children's homes, and this year
I picked you, because I knew you'd be waiting up for me."
"Really?" Melinda asked. "How did you know that?"
"Oh, sweetheart, Santa knows everything," he said.
"I even know what size slippers your Grandma wears —
and what color she likes." With that he gave Melinda
a great big wink, pulled a beautifully wrapped box
from his sack, and placed it under the tree.
"You know my Grammy's *favorite color?*" Melinda was
amazed. "How could you find out stuff like *that?*"
Santa smiled. "Remember . . . I've known
Grammy since she
was *your* age."

Melinda thought about this for a long while as Santa placed more gifts next to the first one. Finally, she said, "Santa, do you really know everything?"

"Yup," he replied. "For instance, I know you have chocolate chip cookies – my favorite kind! – and a glass of milk for me . . . but you forgot to put them out. You left them in the kitchen."

"Oh, my goodness, you're right!" Melinda cried. "I'll go get them right now!"

When she returned, all the gifts had been placed under the tree, and Santa was sitting in the big comfy chair by the fireplace.

"Thank you, sweetheart, I'm really going to enjoy these. I'm sure I won't leave a single one behind."

"Oh, please *do*," Melinda pleaded. "Please leave just *one behind!*"

"What an unusual request," Santa said.

"It's so I can know that you were *really here*," she explained. "It'll be our secret signal."

Santa's face lit up. "Why, what a perfectly yummy idea!"

Then Melinda said, "So if you know *everything*, can I ask you any question at all?"
"Any question at all," Santa nodded.

Melinda thought of every question she'd ever wanted to ask of Santa Claus.

"How do you get to every house in the world in one night?" she suddenly blurted.

"Simple – I stop time," he replied.

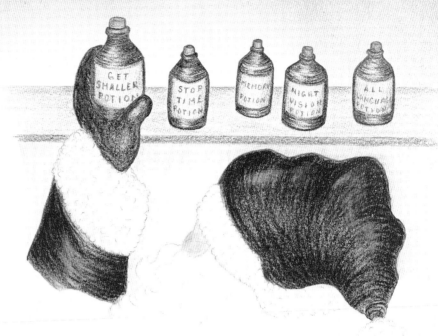

"Oh," Melinda said, almost to herself. "I never thought of that."

"Well," she then asked, "How do you get down the chimney when you are so big and the chimney is so small?"

"Easy," he said. "I just make myself smaller."

"Oh," Melinda said again. "I never thought of that, either."

"But what if the house doesn't *have* a fireplace?" she wanted to know. "How do you get in?"

"Why, then I just use the front door," Santa chuckled. "Although it's not nearly as much fun."

"Okay, tell me this," Melinda said. "How do reindeer fly?"

"They dine on a magic soup that Mrs. Claus prepares."

"Where's the North Pole?"

"Way up north, where there is so much snow it is entirely hidden!"

"How many elves are there?"

"Not as many as people think. They're very rare."

"How many children are getting coal in their stocking
this year because they were bad?"

"None."

"None?" Melinda could hardly believe it!

"Nope. Not one," Santa replied, and then he explained.
"You see, Melinda, there is no such thing as a
'bad' boy or girl. Sometimes children do
things that they wish they hadn't done –
just like adults – but that doesn't make
them bad. It just means they forgot
themselves for a moment."

Santa certainly had some
good answers, and
Melinda was almost out of
questions. But then she remembered
the most important question of all.
It was a question she'd always wanted answered.

"Santa," she began . . . "Who is the real God?"

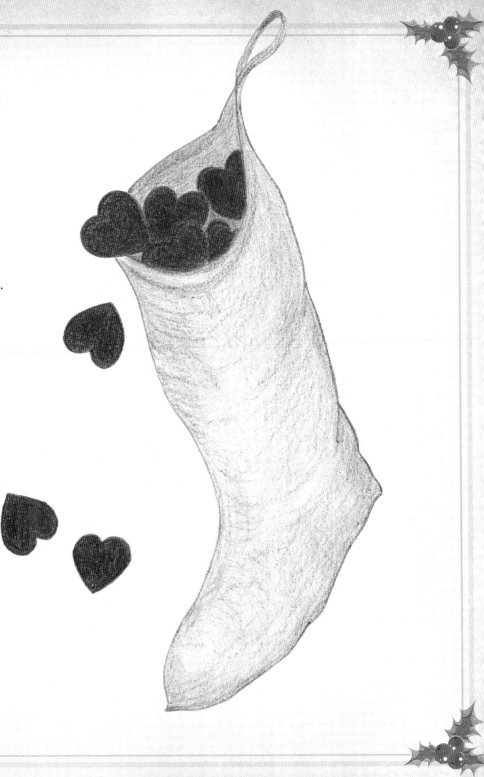

Santa almost
dropped his cookie!

"My goodness," he said,
"that's a pretty big
question for such a
little person.

It could be the
biggest question ever.
What is it that made
you ask Santa that?"

"My friends dared me to,"
Melinda explained as she plopped
right into Santa's lap. "When I
told them that I was certain I was going to
see you tonight they all said, 'Yeah, sure! If you
want us to believe that you actually talked
to Santa, you have to ask a question that only
Santa can answer! Then tell us what he said.'"

"I see," Santa said, stroking his beard.

"So I thought I'd ask you about God, because
some of the kids in my school pray to
Allah . . . some to Jehovah . . . some to
Jesus . . . some to Krishna . . . some to
Yahweh . . ." Her voice got real soft.

"Santa, which God do *you* pray to?
Which God is the real one?"

Who is *Santa's* God?

Santa had been asked many questions by many children in many places for many years, but no one had ever asked him a question quite like *this*. So Santa had to think for a moment about how to answer. Then he remembered something he had seen above the fireplace when he first got to Melinda's house. "What's over there on the mantelpiece?" he asked.

"That's my daddy's collection of Santa Clauses," Melinda smiled proudly. "He's got one from almost every country in the world, and now they're all over the house! On the mantel, on the window sills, *everywhere*."

"Can you tell me about them?" Santa asked.

"Sure," Melinda said, "but what about the question I asked *you?*"

"Oh, I'll answer that for sure," Santa promised. "But I'm just *curious* about these little statues." Then he pointed to one and said, "Who is this?"

"Oh, that's St. Nicholas," Melinda chirped. "He's one of my favorites! He was a bishop in a city called Myra, which is now named Demre." She paused. "That's in Turkey," she added.

"My, you sure know an awful lot about him," said Santa, who was very impressed.

"My daddy tells me the story of each Santa every Christmas," Melinda explained, "and I've practically memorized them! Anyway, Nicholas was so nice to so many people that they made him a *saint*. He was very generous and gave gifts to people in need. They say he even performed miracles, and all of the miracles had to do with giving gifts!"

"And this one here?" Santa asked, looking at another little statue.

"That's Père Noël. He brings presents for all the boys and girls in France!"

And then Melinda pointed to the other Santas one-by-one.
"And that's Weihnachtsmann, from Germany. And that one is Dutch and is called Sinterklaas. Then there's . . . Julemanden from Denmark . . . and Swiety Mikolaj from Poland . . . Father Christmas from England . . . Samichlaus from Switzerland . . . and –"

Dear Santa,

"– Whoa!" said Santa. "You really DO know them all!"

Melinda beamed. "Now *this* one is Santa Kurohsu from Japan, and Joulupukki from Finland, and Santy from Ireland, and Sveti Nickola from . . ."

Santa couldn't stop himself from interrupting. "There are so *many!*" he exclaimed.

"Yes!" Melinda agreed.

A puzzled look crossed Santa's face. "Then," he said slowly, "how do you know who to send your Christmas List to? Which one is the *real* Santa?"

Melinda just sat there for a moment, not knowing what to say.

Then she jumped up
quite suddenly,
because the greatest
idea had just come to her!
Imagining *herself* as
Santa, she exclaimed . . .

"They're ALL the real Santa Claus! They're all YOU! You just *dress* differently,
and call yourself by different *names*, when you're in different *places!*"

"Hmmm," said Santa, "Now why do you suppose I would do that? Why not just look the same and have the same name wherever I go?"

"Because!" said Melinda.

"Because why?" asked Santa.

"Because you want the people in all those different countries to know you when they see you. So you dress just the way they do . . . and *they* give you a name *they* like, and you say, 'Wonderful! Call me whatever you want!'"

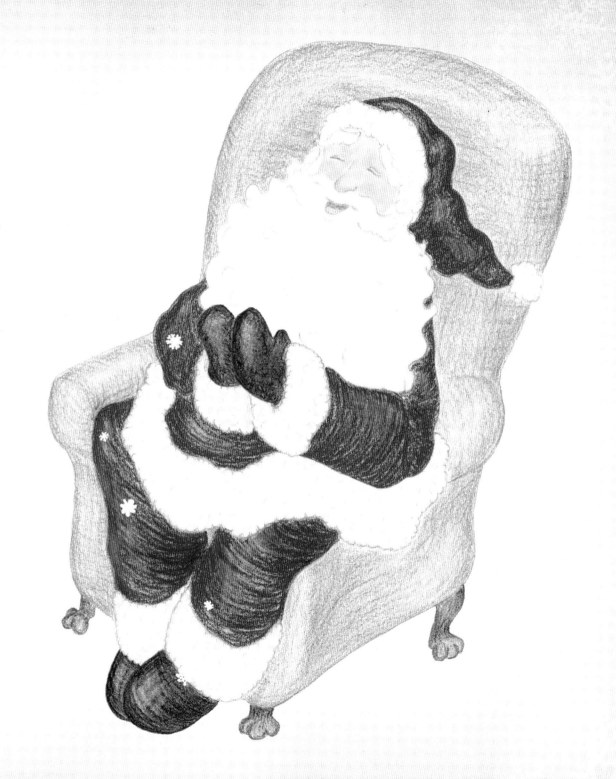

Santa stood up and looked
down tenderly at the
little girl in front of him.

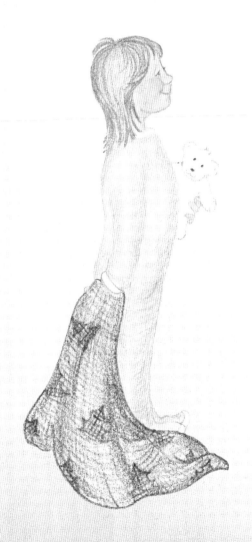

Then, finally, he said,
"You are right, Melinda.
That's very wise of you,
and you are exactly,
perfectly, absolutely right."

Melinda felt very proud
and very happy.

Santa had asked her a really
hard question, and she
had figured out the
answer all by herself!

"Now I have something
special to tell you,"
Santa said, and he bent
down and whispered
in her ear . . .

Would you like to know
what Santa said?

"It's the same way with God."

"Wow . . ." said Melinda quietly.
She had never thought
of that for *sure*.

Now maybe it was all the excitement
at actually meeting Santa, or
maybe it was all those questions
and answers, but just then Melinda
became very sleepy. In fact, she
could hardly keep her eyes open.

"Perhaps it's time for you to go to
sleep now," Santa suggested.
"After all, you have a busy morning ahead."

Then he gently picked her up
and carried her to her bedroom.

"Goodnight, honey," Santa said, tucking her in.

"Night-night, Santa. Thanks for talking with . . ."

But that was all Melinda managed to get
out before she fell fast asleep.

When Melinda awoke,
she raced to the living
room, and there were all
the gifts, neatly arranged
under the tree for the
entire family.

Everything that happened
during the night now
seemed so fuzzy to her.
Did Santa really come,
or did Mommy and
Daddy put those
presents there?

Melinda quickly turned and looked
to the table next to the big comfy chair.
There was the cookie plate and the milk
glass . . . both empty. *Empty.* Not a
single cookie there! Just crumbs!
No cookie left for her!
No special signal!

Melinda almost broke into
tears. *Mommy and Daddy
came down and ate the
cookies just to make it
look like Santa was here,*
she muttered to herself.

Melinda had never
been so sad in her
whole entire life.

Then she happened to glance at the
mantelpiece and she noticed
something strange . . . the Santa Claus
from her country was *not there!*

Her eyes darted frantically around the room.
Then she saw it.

The Santa statue was
nestled on a branch in the
middle of the Christmas tree!

And there, leaning up
against the statue, was . . .

. . . one chocolate chip cookie.